SEAS AND OCEANS

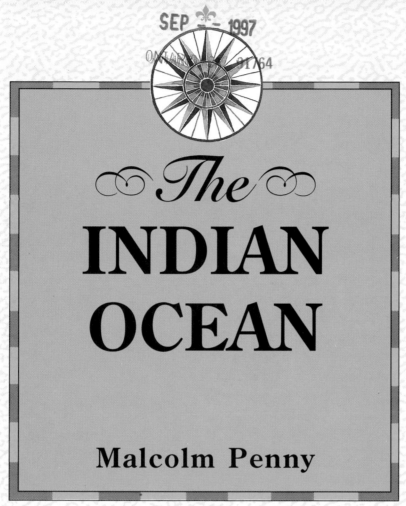

The INDIAN OCEAN

Malcolm Penny

RSVP

RAINTREE Steck-Vaughn
PUBLISHERS
The Steck-Vaughn Company

Austin, Texas

Seas and Oceans series

The Atlantic Ocean
The Caribbean and the Gulf of Mexico
The Indian Ocean
The Mediterranean Sea
The North Sea and the Baltic Sea
The Pacific Ocean
The Polar Seas
The Red Sea and the Arabian Gulf

Cover: Stilt fishermen in Sri Lanka

© Copyright 1997, text, Steck-Vaughn Company

Published by Raintree Steck-Vaughn Publishers, an imprint of Steck-Vaughn Company

Library of Congress Cataloging-in-Publication Data
Penny, Malcolm.
The Indian Ocean / Malcolm Penny.
   p.   cm.—(Seas and oceans)
   Includes bibliographical references (p.   ) and index.
   Summary: Examines various aspects of the world's third largest ocean, covering its geographic features, plant and animal life, human inhabitants, natural resources, and environmental problems.
   ISBN 0-8172-4514-6
   1. Indian ocean—Juvenile literature.
   [1. Indian ocean.]
   I. Title. II. Series: Seas and oceans (Austin, Tex.)
GC721.P46 1997
551.46'7—dc20   96-40996

Printed in Italy. Bound in the United States.
1 2 3 4 5 6 7 8 9 0 0 01 00 99 98 97

Picture acknowledgments:
Finn G. Anderson 36; Axiom 45 (Chris Bradley); Britstock IFA *cover* (Tetsuo Sayama); James Davis Travel Photography 5 (both), 7, 21, 23, 26, 31; Dieter Betz 16, 17; Ecoscene 13 (W. Lawler); Mary Evans 19, 28, 33; Robert Harding 41; Impact 15 (top/Dominic Sansoni), 34 (Christopher Cormack), 37 (Javed Jafferji); Frank Lane Picture Agency 18 (bottom/C. Carvalho), 43 (Eric and David Hosking), 44 (Ian Cartwright); Life File 29 (Gina Green), 38 (Bob Harris); Oxford Scientific Films 10 (Charles Tyler), 20 (Pam and Willy Kemp), 30–31 (top/Javed Jafferji); Panos Pictures 22 (Dominic Sansoni), 33 (Dominic Sansoni), 39 (Dominic Sansoni); Papilio Photographic 18 (top), 24 (John R. Jones), 25 (John R. Jones), 27, 42 (John R. Jones); Photri 35; Science Photo Library 40 (Peter Ryan); Tony Stone Worldwide 14; Wayland Picture Library 6 (Jimmy Holmes), 9 (Jimmy Holmes), 30; Zefa 8 (Tom Van Sant). All artwork is produced by Hardlines except Peter Bull 15 (bottom).

Contents

Words that appear in **bold** in the text can be found in the glossary on page 46.

INTRODUCTION
A Tropical Paradise

In travel brochures, the Indian Ocean appears as a tropical paradise, with palm-fringed islands, **coral** reefs, and turquoise **lagoons**, but there is much more to it than that. The Indian Ocean is the world's third largest ocean, covering 18,528,000 sq. mi. It is an ocean of extremes—straddling the equator, this huge body of water stretches from subtropical waters at 30 °N to meet the icy waters of the Antarctic Ocean.

The Indian Ocean is bordered by the continents of Africa, Australia, and Asia. The exact boundaries of the Indian Ocean are the subject of much argument among geographers. Although the border with the Atlantic is generally agreed,

Right: Ancient granite rocks and white beaches of coral sand make the beautiful islands of the Seychelles a popular tourist destination.

Below: This map shows the main fringing seas, nations, and rivers of the Indian Ocean region.

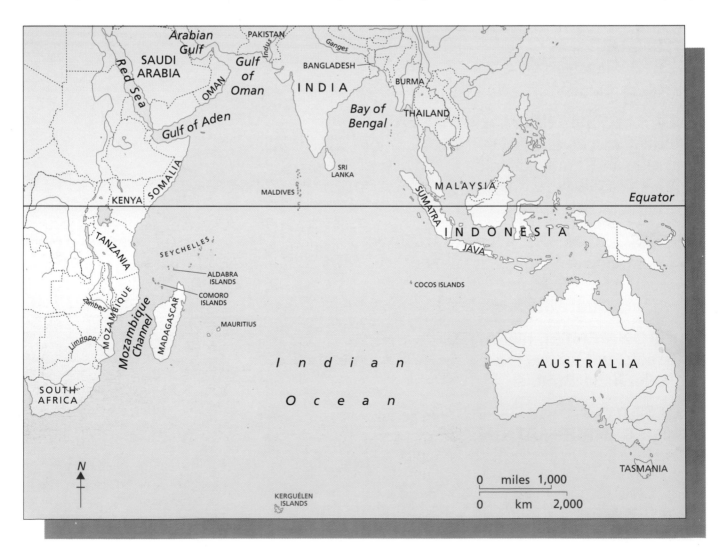

from Cape Agulhas at the southern tip of Africa south along the 20 °E meridian, the Pacific boundary is less clear. It runs north from the Antarctic Ocean along the 147 °E meridian to the South East Cape on Tasmania, and then the boundary becomes controversial.

All oceans are surrounded by seas, but the Indian Ocean has the fewest. The Red Sea and the Arabian Gulf are clearly part of it, as are the fringing Arabian and Andaman seas. The rest of the surrounding waters are large bays, such as the Great Australian Bight.

The Indian Ocean has only a few large islands, but many small ones, some **continental** in origin and others coral or **volcanic**. Many of these islands have played their part in the ocean's long history as a trade route and as a highway for the movement of peoples and cultures. The most extreme example of **migration** is the Malagasy people of Madagascar, who crossed the ocean all the way from Indonesia.

Bombay is one of the great ports of the Indian Ocean. The arch, known as The Gateway to India, was built when India was part of the British Empire.

5

Origins and Coastline

The shape of the world's oceans and continents has not always been the way it looks today. Whole continents have moved around and broken up, forming seas and oceans. The Indian Ocean formed when an ancient **supercontinent** called Gondwana broke up, between 160 and 45 million years ago. Africa drifted northwest and India north on its way to collide with Asia. The crumple zone that resulted from this collision is now the Himalayan mountain range. As India and Africa drifted apart, two crumbs of land were left between them—a large one that became Madagascar, and a tiny one that became the Seychelles. Because they are made of continental rocks, the Seychelles are sometimes called a microcontinent. Australia then moved slowly northeast away from Antarctica, leaving the expanse of water that is now the Indian Ocean.

The coasts of the Indian Ocean are very varied. Some are gentle slopes, caused by **erosion** by the sea and deposits from rivers flowing into them. Wide, shallow **deltas** spread out across the seabed off the coast of Bangladesh, producing

Gently sloping beaches, protected by coral reefs, make ideal settings for fishing villages. This one is near Kovalam, in southern India.

Huge bays and a smooth shoreline show that the western coast of Australia has been weathered by the sea for many millions of years.

low-lying land that is often flooded by storms or swollen rivers. The Indus and Ganges rivers carry the largest amounts of **sediment** to the Indian Ocean. In Southern Africa, the Zambezi River brings sediment to the ocean near Madagascar.

Tropical shores have fringing coral reefs, with a shallow lagoon inside that is often filled with **silt**. Where faults have broken the land away, for example, along the southern shore of the Arabian Peninsula, there are sheer cliffs dropping straight into the sea.

The shores of the Indian Ocean are typically smooth in outline, gently indented, with no areas of **fiords**, such as those seen in Norway or New Zealand. Huge, curved bays, such as the Great Australian Bight, indicate that the shores are very old, weathered, and eroded by the sea over millions of years.

The Ocean Bed

Recent scientific studies, including measurements from satellites, show the bed of the Indian Ocean to be a very complex area of the earth's surface. The flat-bottomed basin is divided by mountain ranges and deep canyons far below the surface of the water.

The **continental shelf** is usually about 62 mi. wide, although between Australia and New Guinea it is continuous, up to 600 mi. wide, and in the Arabian Sea and the Bay of Bengal it extends to nearly 186 mi. The outer edge of the continental shelf is between 148 and 590 ft. deep, although off northern Australia it falls to 2,000 ft.

The Indian Ocean seen from a satellite. The snowy ridge of the Himalayas was raised by the collision of India with the rest of Asia millions of years ago. Beneath the water's surface lie many mountains and canyons.

The vast, muddy delta of the Indus River is often flooded by storms. The silt that comes down the river spreads far out across the seabed.

Beyond the continental shelf, the seabed falls steeply, to between 15,000 and 16,500 ft. Near land, sediment from the skeletons of microscopic creatures has produced a smooth, level area (the abyssal plain). Nearer the center of the ocean the newer parts of the ocean floor have less sediment, and the rough and uneven bottom is called the abyssal hills.

The abyssal plains are often cut by deep-sea channels, only a few miles wide but up to 1,550 mi. long, with raised edges or levees up to 590 ft. high. Underwater rivers of flowing sediment form these channels. Close to the coast, sediments from the shore fall in a smooth slope to the bottom of the continental shelf. Where great rivers flow into the sea, their sediment spreads out in deltas. The Indus and Ganges deltas reach hundreds of miles across the abyssal plains of the Indian Ocean.

Scattered across the otherwise-smooth bottom are a few huge **seamounts** that can reach the surface, and many small volcanic hills, not usually more than 1,500 ft. high. They are tiny features compared with the great mountain ranges that divide up the floor of the Indian Ocean.

PHYSICAL GEOGRAPHY
Mountains and Canyons

The floor of the Indian Ocean is divided by four oceanic ridges—huge, underwater mountain ranges radiating from a center near the Seychelles. To the north lies the Carlsberg Ridge, sweeping southwest is the Southwest Indian Ridge, and diving toward Australia are the Mid-Indian and Southeast Indian Ridges. Some of the mountains in these underwater ranges rise more than 9,800 ft. from the seabed. Each ridge is broken by many **fracture zones**. Some of these zones are 93 mi. wide and 1,800 mi. long, left over from massive undersea earthquakes long ago.

How big and how deep?	
Width	6,696 mi.
North to south	6,820 mi.
Area	18,528,000 sq. mi.
Average depth	15,000–16,400 ft.
Deepest point (Amirante Trench)	29,500 ft.

In 1962, oceanographers discovered a new ridge, called the Ninety East Ridge, running directly south from the Bay of Bengal for nearly 3,100 mi. This ridge has no large fracture zones, suggesting that it is quite young, and it represents movements of the seabed long after those that originally opened the ocean.

The mountainous island of Java is volcanic, and many of its volcanoes are still active. This is Mount Bromo, in eastern Java.

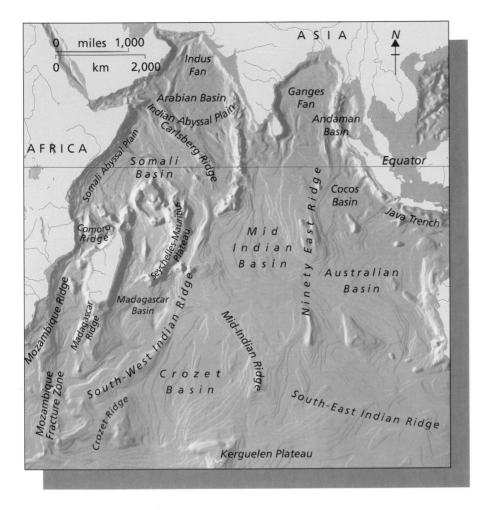

The bed of the Indian Ocean shows its turbulent past, with mountain ranges broken by massive earthquakes.

At its northern end, the Ninety East Ridge comes close to the Andaman Basin, on the edge of the continental shelf near the Malay Peninsula. Curving southeast from here is the Java Trench. South of Java, in the trench, is the second deepest point in the Indian Ocean, measuring 23,375 ft.

Alongside the Java Trench is a long curve of islands called the Sunda Arc. It stretches more than 3,100 mi. from Burma to Australia. The Sunda Arc contains Sumatra, Java, and the Lesser Sunda Islands, including Timor, along an inner ridge. The arc also contains groups of small islands to the north of Sumatra, including the Andamans and Nicobars, on their own shallow ridge.

Madagascar, Seychelles, and the Kerguelen Islands stand on plateaus that are thought to be remains of the original **tectonic plates**—the so-called microcontinents. There is another such plateau off the west coast of Australia that is now underwater. These ancient parts of the earth's crust are too deep-rooted to suffer from major earthquakes.

PHYSICAL GEOGRAPHY
Winds, Tides, and Currents

The open Indian Ocean has two tides a day, usually quite small, although at Aldabra in the west the **tidal range** is about 6 ft. at **spring tides**. Around the coasts the average is 20 to 60 in., although in parts of the Arabian Sea, the Bay of Bengal, and some bays in northern Australia spring tides may reach 26 ft. or more.

Most currents in the northern Indian Ocean, as far as 10 °S, follow the seasonal winds. From May to October, strong southeast **trade winds** across the southern part of the ocean swing around north of the equator to become a southwest **monsoon** heading for India. Within 10 ° either side of the equator the Monsoon Current races eastward, at about 16 in. per second. The currents in the Arabian Sea rotate clockwise at this time of year, while in the Bay of Bengal they travel in a counterclockwise direction.

From November to April the northeast monsoon blows more gently, swinging around to become a northwest trade wind south of the equator. The Monsoon Current flows westward, and the Arabian Sea currents reverse their direction. Only the Bay of Bengal stays the same, turning counterclockwise.

South of 10 °S the currents are constant, forming a pattern known as the Southern Tropical **Gyre**. The Tradewind Current sweeps to the west, the Agulhas Current south from South Africa, the South Indian Ocean Current east at about 30 °S, and the West Australian Current moves northward, to complete the gyre.

Currents in the northern Indian Ocean change with the season; in the south they are constant year-round.

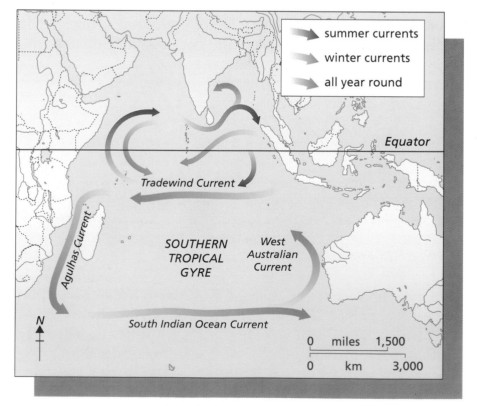

summer currents

winter currents

all year round

Equator

Tradewind Current

Agulhas Current

SOUTHERN TROPICAL GYRE

West Australian Current

South Indian Ocean Current

N

| 0 | miles | 1,500 |
| 0 | km | 3,000 |

The northern currents helped people to sail around the shores of the Indian Ocean in historic times. More important today are the winds that drive these currents, bringing monsoon rains to the Indian subcontinent. The Southern Tropical Gyre became valuable during the 19th century as a route for trading ships traveling between the Far East, Australia, and Europe.

Monsoon winds influence the currents in the Indian Ocean and bring reliable heavy rains to countries in their path. This is the rain forest of Sumatra.

Temperature		
North of 20 °S		
Maximum temperature	Bay of Bengal	82°F
Minimum temperature	Cape Caseyr, Somalia	71°F
South of 20 °S		
Surface temperature		
20 °S	71–75°F	
30 °S	63°F	
40 °S	53°F	
50 °S	43°F	

PHYSICAL GEOGRAPHY
Indian Ocean Islands

There are three types of islands in the Indian Ocean —continental or granitic, volcanic, and coral.

Madagascar, at 226,597 sq. mi., is the fourth largest island in the world, after Greenland, New Guinea, and Borneo. It is separated from Africa by the Mozambique Channel, 500 mi. wide, and more than 9,842 ft. deep for most of its length. Madagascar is a continental island, a fragment of Gondwana separated from Africa as India swung away to the north. Between them is another small continental relic, the Mascarene Plateau, which breaks the water's surface at its northern end as the central Seychelles, the only oceanic granite islands in the world.

At the southern end of the Indian Ocean are two old volcanoes. They might have erupted around the time Gondwana broke up. Today, they are the islands of Mauritius and Réunion. Between Madagascar and Africa are some volcanoes that grew after the breakup of Gondwana and

Left: Moroni, on Njazidja, is the capital of the Comoro Islands. Njazidja is the largest and oldest of the four volcanoes in the island group. The black rock in the picture is made up of volcanic material.

Right: The formation of an atoll

became the Comoro Islands. The oldest, Njazidja, is an extinct volcano with an active cone within it. Mwali and Nzwani, to the southeast, are younger, and the youngest of all is Mayotte. The volcanic activity that formed the Comoro Islands moved from northwest to southeast over many thousands of years.

It is possible to judge the age of volcanic islands by the shape of their coastlines. Young islands have jagged outlines, until they are worn smooth by centuries of erosion by the sea. The beaches on Mayotte are black, made of weathered particles of lava.

Where a volcano comes close to the surface of the ocean, coral grows and eventually forms an **atoll**. The outer Seychelles are mostly made up of coral, as are the Maldives, the Chagos Archipelago, and the Andamans and Nicobars in the northeast.

Madagascar, the Seychelles, and some of the other remote islands have been cut off for so long that they contain plants and animals found nowhere else in the world.

Fragments of an atoll rim form tiny islands in the Maldives. They are perfect for vacation resorts, now the basis of an important industry.

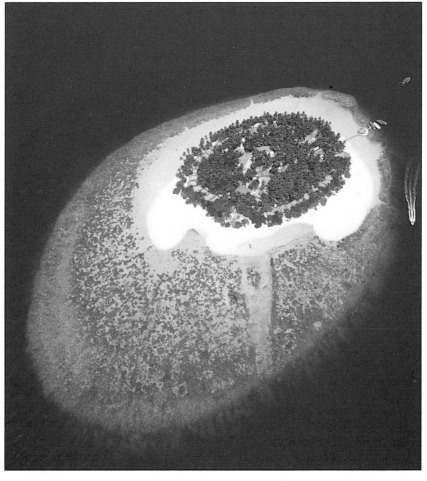

An underwater volcano may erupt to form an island.

Over time the island gradually sinks. If the ocean is warm enough, coral may start to grow around the volcano.

The coral continues to grow up toward the light, and the island sinks below sea level, leaving an atoll surrounding a lagoon.

Mangroves and Their Inhabitants

Mangrove swamps are found on muddy shores in warm climates, at the mouths of great rivers, or around low-lying islands. Mangroves are trees that grow in seawater, producing floating fruits that drift across the sea to grow on other shores. They grow in suitable places from northern Australia to the coasts of Africa, India, and Indonesia and around the many islands in between.

A mangrove swamp shelters an enormous variety of animals. Seabirds and herons nest in tree branches, along with insects and lizards. Crabs and schools of little fish feed on **detritus** trapped among the tangled roots as the tide rises and falls. Mangrove swamps have been called "the nurseries of the sea" because they are so important as refuges for growing fish **fry**. In a few remote places, sea cows and saltwater crocodiles

With its shallow water, plenty of food for fish, and a convenient place to perch, a mangrove swamp is a perfect habitat for herons.

still survive in channels among the trees. But where people have taken over, these large animals have been wiped out—the sea cows as food for people and the crocodiles through people's fear of them.

Mangrove wood is valuable to people because it is used for fuel, and it is resistant to termites, the white ants of the tropics that eat wooden houses and furniture. Because of this, vast areas of mangrove swamps have been cut down for fuel for cooking fires and for carpentry. The swamps are also cleared to make way for coastal development.

Mangroves have another value, often recognized too late. The swamps act as breakwaters, protecting the land from storms and tidal waves. Where the trees have been felled, floods can reach far inland. For example, in Bangladesh, serious floods happen almost every year in the Ganges Delta. Flooding is made worse because forests in the catchment area in the foothills of the Himalayas have also been felled, so that they no longer hold back the monsoon rains. When a flooded river meets a high tide in low-lying farmland crowded with people, the result is a disaster.

Weighing in at around 1 ton and growing up to 26 ft. in length, saltwater crocodiles are the biggest species of crocodiles.

Birds and Land Mammals

The Indian Ocean has a large and varied population of seabirds living and breeding on its many islands. Boobies and frigate birds nest in remote mangrove swamps, and tropic birds and shearwaters dwell on rocky islands where rats have not yet arrived to prey on them. Before humans **colonized** the islands, there were few predators on land, so the birds were quite safe. On some low-lying coral islands in the Seychelles, there are still huge breeding colonies of sooty terns. Local people collect the eggs to eat, but they are careful to leave enough for the colonies to survive year after year.

The islands shelter some of the rarest land birds in the world, and many of them are also among the most endangered species. On the remote atoll of Aldabra lives the Aldabra rail, the last surviving flightless bird of the Indian Ocean, where the dodo and the solitaire were wiped out many years ago. In the Seychelles there are 12 species of birds that are found nowhere else, including the brush warbler, the magpie robin, the paradise flycatcher, and the black parrot, each of which survives only on one or two islands. Madagascar also has its own distinctive birds, though most of them are related to African species.

Above: The word lemur *means "ghost." Most lemurs come out at night, but ring-tailed lemurs such as this one are active during the day.*

Left: The white-throated rail, the last surviving flightless bird of the Indian Ocean, is being closely studied by scientists on the atoll of Aldabra.

The fate of the dodo

The dodo, a large, flightless pigeon, lived for thousands of years on Mauritius, not needing to fly because it had no enemies. When passing sailors discovered that the birds were fearless and could be clubbed where they stood, they slaughtered dodos to supplement their diet of fresh fish and stale flour. The sad fact is that dodos were not very good to eat, just very easy to kill. The last dodo was seen alive in 1681. Its relatives, the solitaires, became extinct on Réunion in 1746 and on Rodriguez in 1791.

The dodo was the size of a turkey, bluish gray in color and very slow-moving. Its name means "sleepy" or "stupid," but on its home island it had nothing to fear until the arrival of humans.

There are very few land mammals on the islands. The Seychelles and Aldabra have bats, which must have been blown there in storms long ago, and on the Comoro Islands lives Livingstone's giant fruit bat, the biggest in the world, with a wingspan of 6 ft. However, on Madagascar there is a unique population of lemurs, **primates** whose ancestors in Africa have long since died out. Sadly, because the forests of Madagascar have been so badly damaged by felling and burning by the crowded human population, most of the lemurs are either **extinct** or seriously endangered.

Fish, Turtles, and Marine Mammals

Much of the tropical Indian Ocean is low in the nutrients that fuel **plankton** growth. Plankton forms the basis of food chains in the ocean, so the Indian Ocean has far fewer fish than the nearby Antarctic Ocean. In the Indian Ocean, large, predatory fish, such as tuna, swordfish, and sailfish travel long distances in search of prey, often disturbing schools of flying fish, which break the surface from time to time. They glide over the waves, their outstretched fins supporting them in the air while their tails drive them along. When they are frightened, flying fish fly toward light. Early sailors used to catch them at night by putting a lantern on deck and waiting for the fish to hit the sail.

This beautiful parrot fish, found near the Seychelles, is displaying its night colors. Parrot fish feed using their beak-shaped mouths to scrape algae and coral from rocks.

On coral reefs, however, the fish population is spectacular in its size and variety. Schools of tiny, brightly colored damsel fish dart among the coral heads; parrot fish, pale blue or pink, crunch the coral with the powerful beaks that give them their name. Butterfly fish and surgeon fish glide past, with glowing patterns of colors and stripes, while groupers and stonefish lie hidden in ambush. Some of the larger reef fish are edible—island people catch them in bamboo basket traps that they set at low tide.

The islands of the Indian Ocean are important breeding places for green and hawksbill turtles. Both species are endangered by hunting—the green turtle for food, and the hawksbill for its shell, known as tortoiseshell. Most of the beaches where the females lay their eggs each year are protected, but illegal hunting still goes on, and the numbers of turtles continue to decline.

Dolphins and porpoises are common, especially in shallower water, and whales are often seen far from land. There was once a small whaling base in the Seychelles, but it closed long ago, and the western Indian Ocean is now an international whale sanctuary. Blue whales and sperm whales may be increasing in number now that they are no longer hunted by humans.

Hawksbill turtles are hunted for their beautiful shells, called tortoiseshell. People use tortoiseshell for making ornaments, but the widespread killing of these creatures means that they are now endangered.

The Maldivians

The Maldives are a group of 1,190 coral islands lying 418 mi. southwest of Sri Lanka. Only 203 of the islands are inhabited. The islands are divided into 19 main atolls, with a total population of 237,000 people. The total land area of all the islands is only 115 sq. mi., and its highest point is 10 ft. above sea level. The capital is the island of Male, with 55,000 inhabitants and an international airport.

The people of the islands are Sunni Muslim. They speak their own language, called Dhiveli, which is a dialect of Sinhalese, the language of Sri Lanka. One word from this language is used all over the world—*atoll*. The people who first came to the Maldives from Sri Lanka, about 500 A.D., were Buddhist. We know this because while digging the foundations of the splendid new mosque on Male in 1984, builders found a huge statue of the Buddha carved from coral rock.

The Maldivians came from Sri Lanka about 1,500 years ago. The Republic of the Maldives became independent from Great Britain in 1965.

From the 14th to the 17th century, during the Ming period, Chinese traders came regularly to the Maldives. Even today, fragments of blue and white Ming porcelain can be found on the beaches. Fishing and growing coconuts for **copra** and **coir** were once the main activities, but they have been replaced by a successful tourist industry, exploiting the beauties of the peaceful islands and their spectacular coral reefs. Tourism is boosted by the use of the old British air force base on Gan Island as a second international airport.

Monsoon storms and **tidal waves** are a constant danger in the Maldives. In 1991 a storm swept across Male, leaving most of the island covered in seawater. Understandably, the Maldivians are very active in studies to warn the rest of the world about the dangers of **global warming** and rising sea levels. Their low-lying islands would be the first country to go under.

The Grand Friday Mosque on Male, capital of the Maldives, was built on the site of an ancient Buddhist temple.

The Sri Lankans

Sri Lanka, formerly called Ceylon, lies east of the southern tip of India, on the other side of the Palk Strait. It is only one tenth the size of Madagascar, at 25,325 sq. mi., but with 17,616,000 inhabitants it has more than 4 million more people. The central part is mountainous, rising to 8,300 ft., surrounded by fertile lowlands that allow the country to support such a dense population.

About half the labor force works in agriculture, growing tea and rubber for export and rice as the staple food crop. It is much more industrialized than Madagascar, with cement

The Temple of the Tooth in Kandy is a place of pilgrimage for all visitors to Sri Lanka.

Lion Mountain

In the center of Sri Lanka is a great fortress, built by King Karyupa in A.D. 477 near the present-day town of Sigiriya. The whole of a small mountain has been sculpted to look like a crouching lion from a distance, with the main entrance to the fortress through its mouth. Its sides are so steep that the top, 590 ft. above the surrounding plains, overhangs the base. On top, palaces and bathhouses have cisterns, or artificial reservoirs, to collect rainwater. The name of the fortress comes from the words *sinha*, meaning lion, and *giriya*, meaning throat.

In the lowlands of southeastern Sri Lanka, there is not much for the cattle to eat until the monsoon brings rain, and the grass grows again.

production, oil-refining, textile production, and food processing among its main activities. A large **hydroelectric** dam is being built on the Mahaweli Ganga, the biggest river on the island, which flows from the central highlands toward the east coast. The average income per person is $540 per year, compared with $230 in Madagascar. Sri Lanka's capital, Colombo, is one of the main ports of southern Asia. About 1.5 million people live and work in Colombo.

An ancient rivalry exists between the Sinhalese people, who form three-quarters of the population, and the Tamils, who live in the northern part of the island. The Tamils want their own homeland, which they call *Eelam*. They have fought for many years, both with Sinhalese extremists and with the government troops who are trying to keep the two sides apart.

In spite of the density of Sri Lanka's population, its forests are far better preserved than those in Madagascar, and very beautiful. Among them are ancient fortresses and temples, dating from the first few centuries A.D. The spiritual capital of the island is Kandy, where a magnificent temple, housing one of Buddha's teeth, is one of the holiest of all Buddhist shrines.

Language and Religion in Sri Lanka			
Language Percentage of speakers		**Religion** Percentage of population	
Sinhala	72%	Buddhist	69%
Tamil	21%	Hindu	15%
Other dialects	7%	Sunni Islam	8%
		Christian	8%

Indian Ocean Explorers

The first people to explore the northern parts of the Indian Ocean were Egyptians, Phoenicians, and Indians, during the first **millennium** B.C. They probably never went out of sight of land, traveling instead around the shores and from island to island. Chinese and Arab navigators explored and established trade routes from A.D. 500 onward. We know that the Chinese traded as far as the Maldives in the 14th century, but medieval Arab and Persian pilots' books describe a route from Sofala in East Africa to China, so there may have been contact across the ocean even earlier.

European involvement began when the Russian voyager Afanasy Nikitin sailed to India from Africa in 1469 on an Indian trading vessel. Close behind him, in 1497, Vasco da Gama employed an Arab pilot at Malindi, on the east coast of Africa, to guide him to the western shores of India. Next came Dutch, English, and French explorers, seeking to establish new trading routes for their countries and setting up new colonies.

Vasco da Gama was selected by the King of Portugal to find a route to India around the Cape of Good Hope. It took him more than a year, but he reached Calcutta in 1498.

The Spaniard Juan Sebastian de Elcano was the first to cross the center of the ocean in 1521, during the first **circumnavigation** of the globe. He took charge after the death of Magellan, the leader of the expedition.

Abel Tasman, the Dutch explorer, explored the northern coast of Australia in 1642–44, and then moved south to reach Tasmania.

The latest great exploration of the ocean took place in 1960–65, in the form of the International Indian Ocean Expedition, involving 20 research ships and hundreds of scientists. They not only explored and mapped the ocean, but also landed on and studied many of the islands, which at the time were virtually unknown.

The rocky coast of Tasmania, named after the Dutch explorer, Abel Tasman, who was the first European to see it, in the middle of the 17th century.

TRAVELERS IN THE INDIAN OCEAN
Trade and Transportation

Coastal people have been trading around the northern shores of the Indian Ocean for at least 3,000 years. There was a regular route from China to Arabia more than 2,000 years ago. The city of Petra was the center of a trading empire from which the Spice Road led across the desert to the Mediterranean and to Europe. As its name suggests, this route carried mainly spices, but silk and jade also traveled this route from Asia. In the other direction, tin and wine traveled eastward.

There are ancient Arab towns on Zanzibar and the coast of East Africa that tell of a long trading relationship. The main goods were spices from Zanzibar and slaves from Africa.

Trade always involves the movement of language and culture. Swahili, the common language of East Africa, is an Arab dialect, and there are Arab words in Malagasy as well. Comorian, the language of the Comoro Islands, is very similar to Swahili, though some of the inhabitants speak pure

Above: Dhows on a beach in Zanzibar. Their design and construction have not changed in 2,000 years.

Right: Islands such as Farquhar, in the outer Seychelles, were once accessible only by trading schooners. Now the islands have airstrips and plenty of visitors.

Left: Battered and over-crowded, ferries such as this one are an important form of transportation around the Ganges Delta in Bangladesh.

Arabic. The spread of Islam followed Arab trade—the people of the Maldives became Muslims in 1153, changing from the Buddhism that they brought from Sri Lanka.

Island hopping and coasting in small vessels allowed early development of these trade routes, but the islands in the middle of the ocean were not colonized until bigger ships were developed and navigation had improved. The Seychelles were known to Arab sailors, and the Portuguese marked them on a map in the 16th century, calling them *As Sete Irmas*— The Seven Sisters. But neither group settled there since there were no inhabitants with whom to trade. The first settlers arrived from the French colony of Réunion in 1770.

As late as 1970, the only access to the Seychelles was by ship, and travel among the Outer Islands (the Amirantes, Aldabra, and the Chagos Archipelago) was by sailing schooner. Then an international airport opened on Mahe, airstrips were built on several of the other islands, and the Seychelles became a popular tourist destination.

The Tea Clippers

Ships called clippers were built in America at the beginning of the 19th century. The name came from their ability to cut (or clip) the time for voyages. Today, it refers to the fast, three-masted, square-rigged merchant ships that were developed for the tea trade with China 50 years later.

Clippers were long and narrow. Their sloping bows and sterns reduced the amount of hull that touched the water. This shape, and the amount of sail they could carry, made them the fastest ships of the time and very beautiful in full sail.

The clippers had to be fast to make a good profit from their cargoes. The first tea to reach Europe each year would get the best price, so the tea clippers would race to deliver the first crop of the season. The journey of 15,900 mi., across the Indian Ocean and around the Cape of Good Hope, could take as little as 99 days, making full use of the trade winds and the Tradewind Current (It was at this time that the winds and currents were named.) The owners of the first ship home made the greatest profit, and the ship's crew was given prize money as a reward.

Ariel *and* **Taeping** *racing up the English Channel, in the last stage of their epic voyage from China in 1866, from a magazine at the time*

The first American clippers raced around Cape Horn to California during the Gold Rush of 1848 and to Australia when gold was discovered there in 1850. Until 1849 the trade to China was restricted to British ships, but when the restriction was lifted, the United States took the lead in building and sailing tea clippers. Then the **depression** of 1857 and the Civil War of 1861–65 caused a decline in American shipbuilding, and the British took over again.

It was a short-lived glory. The Suez Canal opened in 1869, and there was no further need to sail all the way around Africa. The tea clippers carried wool from Australia for a few years, but they were soon displaced by bigger ships with steel hulls that were slower but much more profitable.

The race to London

The greatest tea race ever took place in 1866, between Foochow in China and London in England. Five ships were involved—the *Fiery Cross* sailed on May 29, the *Ariel*, *Taeping*, and *Serica* on May 30, and the *Taitsing* on May 31. The winner was the *Taeping*, which docked in London at 9:45 P.M. on September 6. However, the *Ariel* docked only half an hour later, and the *Serica* an hour and a half after her. The race was so close that the crews' prize money was divided among them. Ironically, so much tea reached London on that day that the price for the first crop of the season was much less than usual.

The best tea is still picked by hand, from the growing tips of the bush, as it was in the 19th century. This tea-picker is working in Sri Lanka.

Military Uses of the Ocean

In the early 18th century, the Seychelles had a very bad reputation, being used by pirates who raided trading ships and retreated to their hideouts in the middle of the ocean. They could cut trees to repair their boats, and there was plenty of food and fresh water. They are also said to have hidden their bounty on shore. Even today, there are people who are convinced that hoards of pirate gold are buried on one or other of the islands.

A satellite-tracking dish on Male, in the Maldives. Global communications make even tiny, remote islands part of the world network.

The development of regular trade routes across the Indian Ocean made the Seychelles important as a place from which the routes could be defended. The islands became a British naval base, and British warships, with French vessels from Mauritius and Réunion, hunted down the pirates.

Diego Garcia Island. The airstrip stretches for the length of the island.

After the great days of commercial sailing ships, the Seychelles became a coaling station for the British navy in World War I, and for a time, there was a small whaling station there. During World War II, the Seychelles was linked with British air force bases on Gan Island, which is part of Addu Atoll in the Maldives, and Diego Garcia in the Chagos Archipelago. Gan became a British air force staging post in 1956 (the modern equivalent of a coaling station) and was handed over to the Maldives in 1976, to become the islands' second international airport. Diego Garcia was handed over to the United States and is still an air base.

In 1968 there was a plan to build a British staging post on Aldabra, a deserted atoll to the north of Madagascar. However, the unique birds of the island, and especially its population of giant tortoises, enabled **conservationists** to argue successfully against the plan. The only other giant tortoises in the world live on the Galápagos Islands.

Copra, Spices, Sugar, and Guano

The islands of the Indian Ocean are ideal for growing coconuts, a valuable commercial crop in the 19th century and into the 20th century. They were split and dried in the sun to make copra, used to make cooking oil and soap. The fibers around the outside of the nut were dried to make coir, which could be twisted into rough rope and woven into coconut matting.

Although coconut production was labor-intensive, wages were low and the trade was profitable for many years. However, artificial substitutes reduced the market for oil and fiber, and the trade dwindled. Most coconuts grown now are for local consumption. The main use for coir today is as a compost for gardens.

The growing of spices was one of the earliest industries, and it is still very successful. Here, too, cheaper synthetic substitutes have been invented, but they are not as good as the real thing. Zanzibar is famous for its cloves, Seychelles grows cinnamon and vanilla, and Sri Lanka produces the best nutmeg and mace.

Coconuts drying in the sun to make copra. Like tea picking, this process has not changed for more than a hundred years, but, unlike tea, it is no longer profitable.

At clove harvest time, the air in Zanzibar becomes filled with the sweet, powerful scent of the drying buds of cloves.

Sugar is another important commercial crop, although in the Indian Ocean only Mauritius has enough land to grow cane in exportable quantities. Elsewhere, it is grown for local use, often to be brewed into a strong alcoholic drink.

Until about 100 years ago, guano (dried seabird droppings) was mined on many of the smaller islands. It is a rich source of nitrate, used in fertilizers and explosives. The guano trade collapsed when the supply ran out. It could not be replaced because mining guano destroys the nesting colonies of the birds that produce it. Also, a chemical way of making nitrate was developed in World War I, when there was a great demand for explosives.

An important product of tropical islands today is perishable crops such as fruit and flowers, which can be flown in a few hours to Europe and to the United States.

Fishing and Tourism

Warm oceans produce fewer fish than cold ones do, but the reefs around the islands provide a reliable source of food for local people, who use traditional traps to catch a wide range of fish. The open tropical Indian Ocean is also quite rich in fish, especially tuna. Deep-sea fisheries have been developed since about 1975, wherever the harbors have enough room for the boats. At first the catch had to be canned for export unless it was frozen and taken away on factory ships, most often to Japan. Canning and freezing facilities on some of the islands now provide jobs for local people. Transporting fresh fish by air has brought more employment and income.

The main method of fishing used in the open ocean is known as longline fishing. Boats lay out lines many miles long, with baited hooks hanging from them. The following day, the boat returns to check the catch. The hooks catch large sailfish

Local fishermen in the Maldives reap the rich harvest of the reefs surrounding their islands. They have to know their trade well, because some reef fish are poisonous and unsafe to eat.

and tuna, but often only the heads remain because the open ocean is full of huge, hungry sharks. Long-line fishing can be very wasteful and destructive. The chief victims are large seabirds, frigates near the equator, and albatrosses farther south. They dive for the bait as the hooks are being lowered and are caught and drowned. One way to prevent this is for the fishing boat to trail streamers in the air as it lays its hooks to frighten away the birds, but not many fishermen take the trouble to do this.

The beauty of the islands and reefs of the Indian Ocean attracts vacationers, whose numbers increase yearly as transportation improves. Islands that have been developed specifically as resorts are an important source of income. It would be ideal if the islands were self-sufficient in food, but too many of the visitors prefer to eat Western food, which has to be imported.

Luxury hotels on perfect, tropical beaches are the basis of a profitable tourist industry. This hotel is in Sri Lanka, but it could be almost anywhere in the Indian Ocean.

Mining Under the Sea

The bed of the Indian Ocean is very rich in mineral resources. Oil and gas reserves are available on the continental shelves, in the Bass Strait, and off Western Australia, as well as the better-known oil fields in the Arabian Gulf and the Red Sea. North of the Western Australian oil fields are large deposits of titanium ore, and the Aghulas Bank off South Africa contains diamonds. Chromium ores have been found in the rift zone of the midoceanic ridge, although there is at present no way of using these deposits.

All over the ocean bed there are huge deposits of manganese nodules. These nodules were discovered in the late 19th century by the first scientists to make a careful study of the beds of the world's oceans, in the research ships *Challenger* and *Albatross*. No one is quite sure how the nodules form, but they are probably the result of a change in the acidity of seawater since the oceans were first formed. Manganese particles sink to the ocean floor, gathering other metals such as copper, nickel, and cobalt as they fall. Because they carry an electrical charge, the particles stick together. The result is small, blackish lumps of crumbly material that would be relatively easy to dredge up from the seabed and process to

Chemical changes in the sea over millions of years have formed nodules of manganese and other valuable metals. We know they are there but have not yet found a way of using them.

extract valuable metals. So far, however, this potentially rich resource has not been commercially exploited.

Manganese nodules are found on the ocean bed all over the world. The exploitation of this resource is still being developed, but already 15,000 tons per day can be dredged up from depths of 19,700 ft. or more. As the technology improves, these deep-sea ores may prove a great resource for the future.

The continental shelf of the Indian Ocean is rich in oil, though some of the deposits are relatively small. This oil platform is off the coast of Sumatra.

ENVIRONMENTAL IMPACTS
Profits and Losses

We have already seen the damage caused to Madagascar's forests by centuries of slash-and-burn agriculture. Many of the smaller islands of the Indian Ocean were destroyed soon after they were discovered, for a quick profit.

Stripping guano from islands that have been seabird colonies for many thousands of years leaves them sterile and useless. One report on these islands proposed that they had a future only as bird sanctuaries, ignoring the fact that removing the guano also removed the trees where the birds nest. Huge colonies of boobies and frigate birds described by early travelers will never return to islands where there are no trees. The profit was short-lived, and the loss is permanent. On Christmas Island, south of Java, the last surviving population of Abbott's booby lives only in a small National Park that protects the last of the forest.

When the forests are gone, the topsoil washes away, leaving gully erosion and infertile red soil. The challenge now is to find a way to restore Madagascar's damaged land.

Felling forests to provide farmland and space for houses endangers native species on islands, but there is another less obvious source of danger. Native island wildlife has evolved in isolation. Some plants and animals are unable to cope with competition or **predation** from alien species introduced by humans. Plants may be slow-growing, never having had to recover from being eaten. When humans arrive, bringing with them predators such as cats and dogs, and herbivores such as cattle, pigs, and goats, their impact can be enormous. Pet birds such as parrots and mynahs can upset the balance of local species, and uninvited guests also arrive with human settlers—rats and mice are the most destructive.

In the Seychelles, where rats were a nuisance in coconut plantations and houses, a biologist suggested introducing barn owls to kill them, a practice known as biological control. The owls were duly brought in from South Africa and went on to wipe out the local population of fairy terns. They left the rats alone, finding the pure white terns easier to catch at night. Looking for a place to breed, the owls took over the nesting places of the native kestrels. Now people are trying to figure out a way of controlling the owls.

The Indian mynah was introduced into the Seychelles as a cage bird. However, some escaped, and now they are a nuisance, taking the eggs and young of the islands' own birds.

ENVIRONMENTAL IMPACTS
Pollution in Paradise

All the oceans in the world are threatened by oil pollution, and the Indian Ocean is no exception. Industrial chemicals and **pesticides** used in **intensive agriculture** cause problems everywhere when they are washed into the sea. Except for these universal pollutants, the Indian Ocean is relatively clean. Around the Amirante Islands, for example, the water over the reefs is among the clearest in the tropics.

However, there are problems even in this paradise. Wreckage or waste from shipping can damage wildlife far from the place where it washed into the sea. Plastic collars from six-packs of beverage cans have been found around the necks of seals and turtles, and seabirds may try to eat floating polyethylene bags, thinking they are squid, with fatal results. Around the

Threats to the Indian Ocean include overcollecting. Collecting coral is banned in most places, in order to preserve the beauty and variety of the coral and its inhabitants.

great harbor cities, such as Mombasa, in Kenya, or Bombay, in India, every kind of pollution has destroyed most forms of life, and the surviving fish cannot be eaten. About the only creatures to benefit are sharks, which feed on garbage thrown into the water and, it is said, on a good number of murder victims.

The islands have problems of their own, many of them arising from the growth of tourism. Sewage disposal is an obvious one, considering the number of visitors and the small size of many of the vacation islands. Another is the chemicals used to control biting flies, which can be a nuisance on beaches. Where land close to the shore has been cleared and leveled to build hotels, sediment washed into the sea can smother the very coral reefs that the hotel guests have come to see. Solving these problems will be the key to the survival of the tourist trade that has become the main form of income for many of the islands of the Indian Ocean.

Storm waves can wash over the low-lying islands of the Maldives. The islands themselves will recover, but the people and their livelihoods are threatened.

Glossary

atoll An island made up of a ring of coral surrounding a lagoon.

circumnavigation Sailing around the world.

coir Coarse fibers from the inside of a coconut's shell.

colonized Taken over by people or animals who have chosen to live in a place.

conservationists People who work to protect the environment.

continental Part of a large landmass. A continental island is one that broke away from a continent as the plates of the earth's surface moved.

continental shelf The area around the edges of a continent that is underwater but not part of the seabed.

copra The dried flesh of coconuts.

coral A rocklike substance made by colonies of small animals such as sea anemones.

deltas Triangular areas of land formed where a river meets the sea on a gently sloping shore.

depression A time of economic troubles and severe unemployment in a country.

detritus Small particles of plants or animals that have rotted and broken up.

erosion Wearing away by water or wind.

extinct No longer alive.

fiords Deep inlets in a mountainous coastline.

fracture zones An area where faults have moved sideways for as much as 200 miles.

fry Young fish.

global warming The continuing rise in the average temperature all over the world.

gyre A large, circular current system.

hydroelectric Electricity generated by the power of running water.

intensive agriculture Farming to produce as much food as possible.

lagoons Shallow seas found inside atolls or between coral reefs and the shore.

migration Traveling from one part of the world to another.

millennium A period of 1,000 years.

monsoon A wind that blows regularly at a particular time of year.

pesticides Chemicals designed to kill animals that are regarded as pests.

plankton Tiny plants and animals that live in the surface waters of the sea.

predation Hunting other animals for food.

primates Animals related to apes and humans.

seamounts Isolated mountains rising from the sea floor.

sediment Rock particles formed by erosion, which settle to the bottom of the sea.

silt A sediment made of very small particles.

spring tides Tides just after new and full moons when there is the greatest difference between low and high water.

supercontinent The name given to the huge landmass that existed before the plates of the earth's crust drifted apart.

tectonic plates The great slabs of rock forming the earth's hard outer layer.

tidal range The difference in height between low tide and high tide.

tidal waves Very large waves caused by earthquakes under the sea.

trade winds The regular and reliable winds across the sea.

volcanic Something caused by the eruption of a volcano.

Further Information

There are very few books about the Indian Ocean itself, so look out for general books about seas and oceans, the countries that lie along the shores of the Indian Ocean and the rivers that flow into it. These are some books that might be useful:

BOOKS TO READ:

Brace, Steve. *Bangladesh*. Economically Developing Countries. New York: Thomson Learning, 1995.

McLeish, Ewan. *Oceans and Seas*. Habitats. Austin, TX: Raintree Steck-Vaughn, 1997.

McNair, Sylvia. *India*. Chicago: Children's Press, 1990.

Nugent, Nicholas. *Pakistan and Bangladesh*. World in View. Austin, TX: Raintree Steck-Vaughn, 1992.

Powzyk, Joyce. *Madagascar Journey*. New York: Lothrop, Lee, and Shepard, 1995.

Waterlow, Julia. *Islands*. Habitats. New York: Thomson Learning, 1995.

Zimmerman, Robert. *Sri Lanka*. Chicago: Children's Press, 1992.

CD ROMS:

Geopedia: The Multimedia Geography CD-Rom. Chicago: Encyclopedia Britannica.

Habitats. Austin, TX: Raintree Steck-Vaughn, 1996.

USEFUL ADDRESSES:

Center for Environmental Education, Center for Marine Conservation, 1725 De Sales Street NW, Suite 500, Washington, DC 20036

Earthwatch Headquarters, 680 Mount Auburn Street, P.O. Box 403, Watertown, MA 02272-9104